the tsunami detectives

Exploring the Science of Tsunamis

sarah michaels

1 /
what is a tsunami?

introduction to tsunamis

HAVE you ever seen a wave while you were at the beach? Imagine a wave that is so big that it is taller than buildings and goes very far onto the beach! This is not an ordinary wave; This is a tsunami (pronounced soo-NAH-mee), also called a "giant wave."

It is one of the most awesome and frightening events that can happen in our world's oceans. Tsunamis are very special types of waves. If you've been to the beach, you know that regular waves can be lots of fun.

Ocean water is continually being pushed around by the wind, creating all sorts of waves. Sets of waves, known as "swell," roll ashore and can be caught by surfers. Tsunamis are very different. They are not caused by the wind, or waves like you see on the ocean's surface. These waves are caused by a sudden change in the ocean, usually the result of an earthquake or volcano eruption.

But in order to understand how a tsunami is created, we have to imagine that the earth is made up of giant puzzle pieces that consist of an outer layer of the earth called the "crust". We call these pieces tectonic plates.

These plates are always moving, pushing against, sliding past or underneath other plates. This continuous motion is called "plate tectonics." Sometimes the plates get stuck and when they finally move, they cause an earthquake. If the earthquake happens under the ocean, the sudden release of energy from the earthquake causes the water to move.

The water begins to go up and down, forming a tsunami. The energy from the earthquake radiates out in all directions. In this way, the energy forms waves that travel across the ocean like cars racing on a track.

A wave can travel through water much faster than a car can drive. Tsunamis can even travel as fast as a jet airplane, over 500 miles per hour. But the most amazing thing about tsunamis is that in deep ocean water, tsunamis are not very high. However, don't be fooled; they contain a lot of energy!

As these waves approach the coast, the water becomes shallower, and do you know what occurs then? The bottom of the wave begins to slow down, but the top continues to travel fast, so much so that the leading wall of the wave is boosted higher and higher.

The small bump in the ocean can generate into a colossal wall by the time it comes crashing down upon the shore. And you might be wondering, how common are tsunamis? Well, they are not an everyday event, but they are more prominent in some parts of the world. The peril is more notable at the rim of the Pacific Ocean, an area that has so many earthquakes that it is dubbed the "ring of fire."

Having said that, they can occur anywhere where there is a robust, unending pool of water, such as an ocean or a significant sea. Scientists invest an enormous amount of time and energy into the study of these killer waves to understand better the occurrence and the science behind them.

They are also equipped with tools and instruments that monitor the movement of Earth's plates and waves in the oceans. So, it often does not land without letting humans know. Scientists are able to detect it hours or even days in advance, before it can wreak havoc, giving people time to find shelter.

The best part is that, despite their ferocity, tsunamis are a natural phenomenon. The more we learn about them, the more secure we can feel in our living environment. For example, if you know what to do when a tsunami is coming, then you can save lives! However, you have to understand how tsunamis work before you can help others.

Also, even though you may be young, you can learn about these waves and make a positive change with the knowledge you possess. Isn't that amazing? You could be the one saving lives, family, and friends by using the knowledge you have gained about tsunamis. However, you have to learn to be able to do that!

Come along with me, and we can learn about our wonderful world and keep underground on what it has to offer!

causes of tsunamis

The sea's silent superheroes — tsunamis! In contrast to villains in superhero movies, tsunamis are not evil forces; they are natural occurrences within the earth. So let's find out what could cause such large waves that sweep across oceans.

Firstly let us discuss about earthquakes which is known as the common cause of tsunami occurrence. In the previous chapter we learned about tectonic plates. Sometimes these great plates move suddenly causing massive shakings called earthquakes. When such tremors occur beneath the ocean surface, they can push water upwards hence leading to formation of waves just like when one jumps into a swimming pool and creates big splashes but this time round it's an entire ocean that gets splashed!

However, not all earthquakes generate tsunamis – it depends on how the plates move. The movement has to be quite dramatic for a tsunami to happen. For instance imagine if you pushed up part of your bedroom floor so that there was sudden bulge; obviously any water above on top side would realise this disturbance and start moving vigorously – same applies undersea where vertical displacement occurs Drain a half-full bottle of water into the sink and watch the water as it spirals down the drain.

The water falling into and displacing the air is a bit like the way a tsunami's waves can lift boats and smash walls. Landslides, which happen both on land and in the sea, are another way tsunamis are created. Slide down a slide on a playground.

Now, imagine a huge amount of rock and earth doing the same thing, sliding into the ocean. A huge splash can send big waves all around. Sometimes big landslides occur because an earthquake runs around shaking the ground, and sometimes big landslides happen all on their own.

But whenever a lot of material suddenly crashes down into the ocean, it displaces the water - or pushes it out of its way - and a tsunami is born.

But it's not just Mother Nature we can blame for these

giant waves. Sometimes, humans can be linked to tsunamis. Very, very rarely, we can be the culprits. Massive explosions and the collapse of huge structures into the ocean can generate tsunamis in much the same way as natural events do, although these human-caused tsunamis are not nearly as common as the natural types. Scientists have all sorts of cool gadgets and technology to help them figure out what causes tsunamis, and to see when and where the next one might occur.

They keep a really close eye on the Earth's crust, monitoring it with extremely sensitive tools that can detect even the tiniest of movements. They also keep watch out over the oceans and the world's many volcanoes using satellites and radars. These things help scientists know if a tsunami is on its way, giving them enough time to alert the public and make sure everyone is out of harm's way. And that's why we're learning about what causes tsunamis.

The better we understand tsunamis, the better we can prepare for them. Like any superhero, we have to understand our enemies so we can try to outsmart them. Scientists learn about tsunamis, how they work, and where they might happen so communities can build walls and plan evacuation routes.

Then, the community practices its tsunami evacuation plan with a drill so that everyone can clear out fast, just in case a tsunami ever does hit! Tsunamis may sound pretty scary, but the more we learn about them, the smarter we can be and the more we can do to live safely, and even happily, in places where a tsunami may happen. And nearly everything we learn about tsunamis can help protect us, and teach us about the natural world and how we live on it. Isn't it cool how the motion of the earth under our feet can send waves across the world's oceans?

As we work to understand all types of waves and the earth beneath our feet, we'll continue to learn more about the ways the earth and the sea, and us, are connected. The better we understand that connection, the more we can understand the planet we live on, its amazing natural power, and all the cool stuff that comes along with it! Keep on exploring and check out the awesome video to learn more!

"did you know?" fun facts about the ocean and tsunamis

Do you want to know how awesome and cool the ocean is, all in one? Does it ever cross your mind how strange and extraordinary it is beneath the ocean's surface? Indeed, it is a secret world, isn't it? So much of the ocean is mysterious and magic, isn't it? And when it comes to tsunamis, those giant waves we mentioned, well, you are going to learn a whole lot about them! Trust us, you are in for a wild ride!

Amazing Ocean Facts

1. The Ocean Is Super Deep!

Did you know that most of the ocean is unexplored? That's right! The average depth of the ocean is about 12,080 feet, which is like stacking more than 2,000 adults head-to-toe. The deepest part of the ocean is called the Mariana Trench, and it's about 36,070 feet deep—deeper than Mount Everest is tall!

2. Water, Water Everywhere!

Oceans cover more than 70% of the Earth's surface. That means most of our planet is underwater. The Pacific Ocean is the biggest and it's so large that all the continents could fit into it with room to spare!

3. Home to Incredible Creatures

The ocean is home to millions of species, and many of them haven't even been discovered yet. There are glowing fish, giant squids, and even sharks that can live for hundreds of years!

4. Underwater Waterfalls and Rivers

Yes, you read that right! There are places in the ocean where denser, saltier water creates currents that flow like rivers. There's even an underwater waterfall between Iceland and Greenland that's much bigger than any waterfall on land.

Terrific Tsunami Facts

5. Not Just One Wave

When you think of a tsunami, you might picture a giant wave crashing into the coast. But actually, a tsunami usually involves a series of waves, and the first one might not even be the biggest. That's why it's always important to stay away from the coast until an official "all clear" is given.

6. Super Fast Waves

Tsunamis can travel at the speed of a jet plane, over 500 miles per hour, when they're out in the deep ocean.

That's faster than you could ever go on your bicycle or even in a car!

7. Tsunamis in Lakes? Yes, It Can Happen!

While we usually hear about tsunamis in oceans, they can also happen in large lakes. If there's a big enough disturbance like a landslide or an earthquake, even lakes can generate tsunamis.

8. Historical Tsunamis

One of the oldest recorded tsunamis happened way back in 479 B.C. in the Greek city of Potidaea. According to historical accounts, it saved the city from a Persian fleet that was trying to invade!

Cool Connections Between the Ocean and Tsunamis

9. The Ocean's Shape Affects Tsunamis

The shape and the features of the ocean floor play a huge role in how tsunamis travel. Underwater mountains and valleys can redirect or amplify tsunamis, making some areas more vulnerable than others.

· · ·

10. Protecting the Coast

Did you know that healthy coral reefs and mangrove forests can help protect the coast from the impact of tsunamis? They act like natural barriers that absorb some of the wave's energy.

11. Tsunamis Help Scientists

Every tsunami, while dangerous, gives scientists a chance to learn more about how our Earth works. They use data from tsunamis to study the ocean floor and improve their models for predicting future waves.

12. Tsunami Stones

In Japan, there are ancient stone markers that warn people not to build homes below a certain point on hillsides. These markers were placed there based on past tsunami experiences, showing that even long ago, people were learning from and adapting to their environment.

2 /
history of tsunamis

famous tsunamis

WHEN WE STUDY TSUNAMIS, it's not just about grasping how these huge waves operate; it's also about reading the tales of tsunamis past that have been seared into history. Reading these stories is essential in learning and planning for the future. So, we're going to take a time machine and journey across the world to catch a glimpse of some of the most infamous tsunamis throughout history.

The Great Lisbon Earthquake Tsunami of 1755

Imagine a sunny morning turning into one of the most tragic days in history. On November 1, 1755, the city of Lisbon, Portugal, was struck by a massive earthquake that nearly destroyed the city. But that wasn't all. Shortly after the earthquake, a huge tsunami rolled in, sweeping up everything in its path. The waves traveled across the Atlantic Ocean and even reached the Caribbean. This event was so significant that it changed the way people built cities and sparked new interest in studying earthquakes and tsunamis.

Krakatoa's Catastrophic Tsunami, 1883

The eruption of the Krakatoa volcano in Indonesia is one of the loudest and most devastating volcanic events ever recorded. The immense power of the eruption generated a series of massive tsunamis that caused destruction along the coasts of Java and Sumatra, claiming the lives of over 36,000 people. The waves were so powerful that they were felt around the world, and the sound of the eruption was heard as far away as Australia and the island of Rodrigues near Mauritius, thousands of miles away.

The Devastating 2004 Indian Ocean Tsunami

On December 26, 2004, an enormous undersea earthquake off the coast of Sumatra, Indonesia, triggered what would become one of the deadliest natural disasters in modern history. The resulting tsunami affected 14 countries around the Indian Ocean, with waves up to 100 feet high. It caused immense destruction and tragically took the lives of over 230,000 people. The widespread impact of this tsunami led to significant improvements in tsunami warning systems around the world.

Japan's 2011 Tōhoku Tsunami

On March 11, 2011, a mega-thrust earthquake known as the Great East Japan Earthquake occurred off the coast of Japan. This powerful earthquake triggered a massive tsunami that reached heights of up to 133 feet and traveled up to six miles inland. The tsunami caused extensive damage to the Fukushima Daiichi Nuclear Power Plant, leading to a nuclear disaster. The world watched in horror, and the event highlighted the need for stringent safety measures in nuclear power plants located near coastlines.

Chile's Double Disaster in 1960

The most powerful earthquake ever recorded struck Chile on May 22, 1960. Known as the Valdivia Earthquake, it registered a magnitude of 9.5 and caused a massive tsunami that affected the entire Pacific Rim. Coastal towns in Chile were devastated, and the waves traveled across the Pacific, causing damage as far away as Hawaii, Japan, and the Philippines. This event led to the creation of the Pacific Tsunami Warning Center, which plays a crucial role in monitoring tsunamis in the Pacific Ocean to this day.

These are the tsunamis of history, and they remind us how small our place is in this big and sometimes dangerous world we live in. Each and every story has lessons to teach us about the immense power of the Earth, the importance of preparedness, and what can be accomplished when people from all walks of life come together to rebuild and heal after disaster strikes.

To know the tsunami is to understand the world is a small and interconnected place. An earthquake in one part of the world can send waves crashing down upon another shore ten thousand miles away. A push of a button or a single stroke of a pen can change the lives of millions halfway around the world. That is why we spend so much time studying these events, so that the next time it happens - and it will- we can better know what to do and where to go.

3 /
how do we detect tsunamis?

warning systems

EVER WONDERED how on earth people know when a tsunami is on its way? It's not like you can just stare out to sea and see it coming with hours to spare. Tsunamis move pretty fast—up to about as fast as a jet plane—so we need to get the word out as soon as we can. There's no point warning people after the waves have struck, so some kind of tsunami warning system is a must. It's like the undiscovered heroes of the story, working behind the scenes to make sure there are no horror movie scenes when a big wall of water comes smashing in. Let's take a look at how these systems operate and how they help save lives.

The Basics of Tsunami Warning Systems

A tsunami warning system is a network of sensors,

computers, and alarms designed to detect tsunamis and alert people as quickly as possible. There are two main types: regional and local systems. Regional systems watch for tsunamis that might affect many countries, like the Pacific Tsunami Warning System that protects countries around the Pacific Ocean. Local systems, on the other hand, focus on specific areas and give very quick alerts to nearby people.

How Do These Systems Detect a Tsunami?

The first line of defense in detecting a tsunami is an earthquake monitor. Since most tsunamis are caused by underwater earthquakes, these monitors can quickly tell if an earthquake has happened—a possible first sign of a tsunami. These monitors are very sensitive and can detect even the smallest quakes!

Once an earthquake is detected, scientists need to figure out if it has actually caused a tsunami. That's where buoys come into play. Buoys are like little floating science labs scattered across the ocean. They can measure changes in the water level and send this information back to scientists using satellites. If the buoys report sudden changes in water height, it's a strong sign that a tsunami might be on its way.

Computer Models and Predictions

After getting data from the earthquake monitors and buoys, scientists use computer models to predict how big the tsunami might be and where it will hit. These models look at the ocean's depth, the shape of the seafloor, and how waves travel to predict the tsunami's path and power. This helps determine which areas need to be warned.

Getting the Word Out

Once scientists know a tsunami is coming, the next step is to alert the people who are in danger. This is done through alarms, which can be loud sirens in coastal areas, or through more modern means like TV, radio, and even mobile phones. In many places, you might get an emergency alert on your phone that makes a loud noise to grab your attention, telling you to move to higher ground.

Local Warning Systems

Some areas with a high risk of tsunamis have local warning systems. These systems can give very fast warnings based on local earthquakes and water level changes. For example, in Japan, the warning system is so advanced that alerts can be sent out within minutes of an earthquake, giving people maximum time to evacuate.

Drills and Education

Having a great warning system isn't enough by itself. People also need to know what to do when they hear a tsunami warning. That's why many coastal towns have regular tsunami drills. These drills teach everyone, from tiny kids to grandparents, how to quickly and safely get to higher ground when they hear the warning.

Continuous Improvement

Scientists and engineers are always working to make tsunami warning systems better. They use lessons learned from past tsunamis to improve their models and make the warning process faster and more accurate. Each improvement can mean the difference between safety and disaster, so this work is super important.

Why Warning Systems Matter

detecting tsunamis before they hit us! modern technology and science help us detect tsunamis and warn people about them more effectively than ever before. these warning systems save thousands of lives by providing time for people to reach safe areas. remember the story about the 2004 indian ocean tsunami?

a lot has changed since then! much better systems are in place so that such a large loss of life doesn't happen again. warning systems are critical tools in the fight against the threats that tsunamis pose. the more we combine technology, science, and community preparedness, the safer we will be from these monstrous waves. with what we learn, we can improve disaster response, recovery, and long-term community resilience. even if a tsunami does strike, it will hit a prepared and resilient community!

technology behind the scenes

Have you ever wondered how we can get word of tsunamis coming our way so quickly? It is almost like there is a superhero team out there, but instead of wearing capes and having superpowers, they are surrounded by gadgets and science, prepared to save the day. So, how does it all work? Here we take a look at the incredible technology that makes it all come together. It is not just a few computers and some alarms, but an entire advanced network of technology that is always looking out for us.

Earthquake Monitors: The First Watchers

The first step in predicting a tsunami is catching the earthquake that might cause it. To do this, scientists use seismographs, which are super sensitive instruments that can detect even tiny tremors from deep within the Earth. These monitors are placed all around the world, and they constantly send data back to various earthquake research centers. Imagine having such good hearing that you could hear a pin drop in another room—seismographs can detect shakes that are much less obvious than that!

Buoys: The Ocean's Sentinels

Out in the vast oceans, special buoys float on the surface, keeping an eye on the water movements. These aren't just any ordinary buoys; they are equipped with technology called pressure recorders that can sense any change in the depth of the water above them. If an earthquake pushes the water up, these buoys notice the change and send a signal via satellite to scientists on land. It's kind of like when you feel the bump when riding a bike on a rough path, but much, much subtler.

Satellites: Eyes in the Sky

Above Earth, satellites keep an eye on the planet, including the oceans. These high-tech space gadgets use radar to detect changes in sea level and unusual wave patterns that might indicate a tsunami. They're like scouts in a watchtower, able to see far and wide, ensuring nothing unusual goes unnoticed.

Computer Models: Simulating the Future

Once the initial data comes in from the seismographs and buoys, it's up to powerful computers to figure out what might happen next. These computers use software that can simulate how waves travel through the ocean, based on the ocean's depth, the shape of the sea floor, and the size of the earthquake. This helps predict not just when a tsunami might strike, but also how powerful it could be. It's a bit like playing a video game where you can see the consequences of your actions before you even take them.

Communication Networks: Spreading the Word

Knowing about a tsunami is only useful if you can tell everyone who needs to know. This is where advanced communication technologies come in. As soon as a threat is identified, warnings go out through various channels—television, radio, internet, and even directly to people's phones. In many coastal areas, there are also loud sirens that sound alarms to let everyone know they need to move to higher ground.

GIS and Mapping Tools: Visualizing the Risk

Geographic Information Systems (GIS) are used to create detailed maps that show which areas are most at risk from a tsunami. These maps take into account the local geography, such as the height of the land and its distance from the coast. They help emergency planners decide where to focus their efforts and can even guide the design of evacuation routes and disaster preparedness plans.

Drones and Robots: The New Explorers

After a tsunami hits, drones and robots can be sent out to explore areas that are too dangerous for people to go. These machines can take pictures and gather data about the damage, helping rescue teams know where they are needed most. Some robots can even go underwater to inspect bridges, ships, and underwater pipelines to make sure they haven't been damaged.

Continuous Learning and Improvement

What's really amazing is that all this technology keeps getting better. Every time a tsunami occurs, scientists learn more about how they behave. They use this knowledge to update their models and improve their equipment, so each warning system becomes more accurate and reliable than the last.

Empowering Communities

With all this technology, communities are better equipped to handle the threat of tsunamis. Schools often have programs that teach kids about tsunami safety, using videos and interactive tools that help them understand what to do if they ever hear a tsunami warning. This way, everyone, from the youngest to the oldest, knows how to stay safe.

how scientists predict tsunamis

Think of a group of explorers keeping an eye out for massive waves while gathering data and observations from the seabed displayed on big screens. It sounds like a scene from a movie but it is happening all over the world right now! Tsunami scientist and researchers around the world are tirelessly working on the best means to monitor, send out warnings and generally keep us safe from these catastrophic waves.

Understanding Earthquakes and Ocean Floors

First things first, scientists need to understand where tsunamis come from. Most tsunamis start with an earthquake under the sea. When the Earth's plates shift suddenly, it can lift the ocean floor and push up a huge amount of water. This is what creates a tsunami. To keep an eye on this, scientists use tools called seismometers that can detect earthquakes as they happen. These tools are super sensitive and can pick up vibrations from deep within the Earth.

But knowing an earthquake has happened isn't enough to predict a tsunami. The earthquake must be the right type (it has to move the sea floor up or down, not just shake it), and it has to be strong enough. Scientists use data about the earthquake, like its strength and the way it moved the Earth, to figure out if it could cause a tsunami.

The Role of Deep-ocean Assessment and Reporting of Tsunamis (DART) Systems

One of the coolest tools scientists use is the DART system. These are special buoys placed in the ocean. Each buoy has a sensor on the ocean floor that can detect changes in water pressure. This change in pressure happens when a tsunami wave passes over. The buoy then sends this information to satellites, and the satellites send it back to Earth, to the scientists waiting for any signs of a tsunami.

Satellites Watching from Space

Satellites play a huge part in tsunami prediction. They orbit Earth and look at the oceans from above. Satellites can detect changes in the height of the ocean's surface. When a tsunami forms, it changes the shape of the ocean surface slightly, even though it's way out at sea and hasn't built into a giant wave yet. Satellites can catch these changes and send the information back to Earth.

Computer Models and Simulations

With all this data from seismometers, buoys, and satellites, what's next? It's time for computer models! Scientists use computer simulations to turn all the data they've gathered into predictions about how big a tsunami might be and where and when it will hit. These models take into account the shape of the sea floor, the coastline, and even how deep the water is.

These models are like video games that can fast-forward to see the future. They help scientists test different scenarios: What if the tsunami is bigger? What if it hits here instead of there? This helps everyone get ready for different possibilities.

Warning Systems and Alerts

Once scientists think a tsunami is on its way, they need to warn people. This part is super important because it's what keeps people safe. Using the predictions from their models, they can send alerts through TV, radio, internet, and cell phones, telling people what they need to do and where they need to go.

Education and Community Drills

Knowing about a tsunami isn't enough; people also need to know what to do. That's why part of a scientist's job is also about teaching and practicing. Many places that are at risk of tsunamis have drills, where everyone practices what to do if a tsunami alert is sounded. Schools teach kids about tsunamis, too, so even the youngest ones know how to stay safe.

Always Improving

The best part about science is that it never stops getting better. Every time a tsunami happens, scientists learn a little more. They use what they learn to improve their predictions and make their models even better. They also work on making their warning systems faster and more clear, so that everyone understands them right away.

A Global Effort

Predicting tsunamis isn't just something one country or one group of scientists does. It's a global effort. Countries around the world share their data and work together. After all, tsunamis don't care about borders, so it takes everyone working together to keep safe.

4 /
what happens during a tsunami?

before the tsunami

PICTURE YOURSELF AT THE BEACH, putting the finishing touches on the biggest sandcastle you have ever built. The sun is shining, the waves are rolling in gently, and all seems right in the world. But while it looks like another perfect day at the shore, big waves might be brewing far out to sea. This is the time that precedes a tsunami, a massive wave generated by undersea disturbances, such as earthquakes. What happens in those few precious hours before a tsunami strikes? Read on to see how humans and technology team together for readiness.

Detecting the Signs

The story of a tsunami begins long before the wave

reaches the shore. Under the ocean's surface, when an earthquake occurs, it can shift the sea floor, suddenly pushing water up and creating waves that travel across the ocean. The first sign of a possible tsunami is usually this type of underwater earthquake. Luckily, we have technology that can detect these quakes the moment they happen.

Scientists use seismographs, which are super sensitive instruments that can feel and record the vibrations from earthquakes. These tools are placed all around the world, both on land and at the bottom of the ocean. When they detect an earthquake that is strong enough and in the right location to possibly cause a tsunami, they quickly send alerts to tsunami warning centers.

Warning Centers Spring into Action

When a potential tsunami-triggering earthquake is detected, tsunami warning centers evaluate the data. They need to act fast, figuring out if a tsunami was really generated and where it might be heading. These centers use computer models to predict how fast the wave is traveling and when it might reach different coastlines.

As soon as they have enough information, the warning centers send out alerts to the public and to emergency agencies. These alerts can be broadcast over TV, radio, and the internet. Even mobile phones might receive urgent tsunami alert messages. In coastal areas, loud sirens might also sound to warn people that they need to move to higher ground.

The Role of Local Observations

While technology does a lot of the work in detecting and predicting tsunamis, local observations are also crucial. People living near the coast are often the first to notice unusual changes in the ocean that could indicate a tsunami. For instance, one surprising sign of an approaching tsunami is when the water at the beach suddenly pulls back much further than normal, exposing the sea floor. This can happen minutes before the tsunami arrives.

Local officials keep an eye on these signs too. They might order evacuations even before they get the official alerts if they think a tsunami is coming. It's all about keeping people safe.

Educating the Community

Knowing what to do before a tsunami hits is a critical part of keeping safe. Many coastal areas have regular tsunami drills and education programs, especially in schools. Kids learn about the signs of a tsunami and what to do if they think one is coming. They are taught to drop, cover, and hold on during an earthquake and to head to higher ground or inland immediately afterward.

Communities also practice evacuation routes and have signs posted to show these paths. These routes are planned to be the quickest and safest way out of areas that might be affected by a tsunami.

Emergency Kits and Plans

Families who live in areas where tsunamis could happen often prepare emergency kits and have a family emergency plan. An emergency kit might include things like water, food, a first aid kit, a flashlight, and a radio. It's all packed and ready to go in case the family needs to leave home quickly.

The family plan includes knowing where to meet if you get separated and who to call. It's important for everyone, even kids, to know these plans well.

Monitoring and Adjustments

Even in the hours before a tsunami strikes, scientists and officials are continuously monitoring the situation. They update their predictions and warnings as new data comes in. If the situation changes, they let people know, whether it's to escalate the warning or to cancel it if the threat passes.

Preparing for a tsunami involves everyone, from scientists and officials to local communities and families. It's about having the right technology to detect and predict tsunamis, the procedures to spread warnings quickly, and the education to know how to respond. Together, these efforts help ensure that when a tsunami does head toward the coast, people are ready to act quickly and stay safe.

during the tsunami

Think of the last time you watched a movie about explorers on a great ocean adventure. As you follow along and look at the magnificence of the oceans, the adventurers suddenly look up to see a wave that is so, so much bigger than everything all around it. That wave is a tsunami and it is extraordinary. In the movies or while your favorite character adventures, it is very exciting. However, in reality, tsunamis are not the least bit fun- and completely mind-blowing. So, how do we protect ourselves in the event of a tsunami?

The Wave Approaches

When a tsunami is about to hit, the first thing you might notice, apart from the warning alarms, is a very unusual sight at the beach. The water along the coastline might pull back far from the shore, exposing parts of the seabed that are usually hidden under the sea. This is a natural warning sign and means the wave is coming soon.

As the tsunami wave approaches, it can look different from normal sea waves. Tsunamis are not like the curling, rolling waves that surfers ride. Instead, they might just look like a rapidly rising tide that doesn't stop coming in. The water rushes over the beach and the land beyond it, gaining height and speed as it goes.

What to Do

If you ever find yourself near the coast and you see these signs or hear a tsunami warning, the most important thing to do is move to higher ground immediately. Don't wait to see the wave; tsunamis move incredibly fast, and every second counts.

Local officials usually know the best evacuation routes, and following their directions is crucial. In many places prone to tsunamis, signs will point you to the safest path to take. It's important to stay calm and move quickly without running or pushing.

During the Tsunami

Once the tsunami hits, the water can push inland for miles depending on the slope of the coast and the size of the wave. This is why moving to higher ground is so important. The power of the water is enormous. It can carry debris, like pieces of buildings, trees, and cars, which can be very dangerous.

If you're indoors when the tsunami hits, stay inside if you're already at a higher level in a sturdy building. Move to the upper floors to avoid being caught in the water. Avoid windows to protect yourself from breaking glass and other flying objects brought by the water.

If You're Caught in the Water

If you find yourself caught in the tsunami water, try to grab onto something that floats. Pieces of debris can be dangerous, but finding a stable floating object can help keep you above the water. Holding on to something also helps you conserve energy and keeps you safer from underwater hazards.

Rescuers advise forming a group if possible. Being with others can increase your chances of being seen and helped. It's also important to keep your mouth closed to avoid swallowing polluted water.

After the Wave Passes

It might seem like it's safe once the first big wave has gone, but tsunamis often come in a series of waves. Sometimes, later waves can be even larger than the first. That's why it's important to stay where you are on high ground until authorities say it's safe to return.

The water from the waves can take a long time to recede, and it can leave behind a lot of mud and debris. Emergency services usually arrive as quickly as possible to help anyone who needs assistance and to make sure it's safe for people to go back to their homes.

Learning from Each Tsunami

Every time a tsunami occurs, scientists study what happened to learn more and improve their predictions and warnings. They look at how fast the waves traveled, how far they reached, and what kind of damage they did. This information helps improve models and plans for future tsunamis.

During a tsunami, the community's strength is tested,

but also shown in full force. Neighbors, friends, and even strangers come together to help each other out. This shows how, even in the face of such powerful natural events, people can make a big difference by being prepared and looking out for one another.

after the tsunami

The sea finally retreats, the leviathan waves that had pounded the coast now no more than fragile ripples breaking on the shore. The tsunami is over and the wave of devastation has ebbed away. But it has left behind something else in its wake. Now we move to the aftermath of a tsunami and the true story of long-term healing, regeneration and recovery of community.

Surveying the Damage

As soon as it's safe, emergency teams spring into action to assess the damage. These teams include firefighters, police, medical staff, and volunteers. They check for injured people and make sure everyone is safe. They also look at buildings, roads, and bridges to see what's been damaged. It's a bit like detectives looking for clues, except they're figuring out what needs to be fixed first.

Electricity and phone lines might be down, making it hard to communicate. Emergency workers use radios and sometimes even satellite phones to coordinate their efforts. It's important to restore communication quickly so that people can reach their families and emergency services can organize their help more effectively.

Helping the Injured and Homeless

One of the first priorities is to help people who are hurt or who have lost their homes. Medical teams set up temporary clinics to treat injuries. These might be cuts, bruises, or more serious conditions caused by the water and debris. Shelters are set up for people who can't go back to their homes. These shelters are often in schools, community centers, or tents. It's like having a big sleep-over, but one that nobody planned.

Cleaning Up

Cleaning up after a tsunami is a huge job. The waves can leave behind a lot of mud and debris, including broken pieces of buildings, trees, and sometimes even boats. Workers and volunteers use trucks, bulldozers, and sometimes cranes to clear the roads and clean up the mess. It's important to clean up quickly to make sure that roads are clear for emergency vehicles and to prevent any accidents from the debris.

Communities often come together to help with the cleanup. It's a way for everyone to pitch in and help get their town back to normal. Kids can help too, by doing things like organizing supplies at a shelter or helping neighbors clean their yards.

Checking for Dangers

Another important step is to check for any new dangers created by the tsunami. For example, the water might have caused gas leaks or chemical spills. Experts come in with special equipment to test the air and water to make sure it's safe. They also look for signs of damaged gas lines or oil tanks, especially near harbors or industrial areas.

Water supplies might be contaminated, so safe drinking water is brought in, and people are told how to clean their water at home until the taps are safe to use again.

Rebuilding and Planning for the Future

Once the immediate emergency is over, the long process of rebuilding begins. This can take months or even years. People rebuild their homes and businesses, and governments repair roads and bridges. It's a slow process, but it's also a time when communities can make improvements, like building stronger buildings that can withstand future tsunamis better.

Scientists and engineers study what happened to learn how they can improve building designs and early warning systems. This way, if another tsunami ever comes, the community will be better prepared, and hopefully, less damage will happen.

Learning and Growing Stronger

Afterward, a community often becomes more united.

There are stories to share about how people saved themselves, others helped out, and the whole town inoculated itself again, building stronger walls and homes at least to the effect that the next hit may not be as disastrous.

Schools may organize classes about tsunamis, perhaps explaining what causes the waves and what to do if one ever hits. It is important to be informed about tsunamis and how to protect ourselves so that if another wave does race ashore, you will know how to react, even if you're still "just a kid."

quiz section: test your knowledge about tsunami safety

Quiz 1: True or False?

Let's start with some true or false questions. Read each statement and decide if it's true or false. Ready? Here we go!

1. True or False: A tsunami is just a single giant wave.

Hint: Think about how tsunamis usually arrive.

2. True or False: Tsunamis can only happen in the ocean near the beach.

Hint: Where else can tsunamis occur?

3. True or False: If you're on the beach and the water suddenly pulls back a lot, it's a good time to explore the sea floor.

Hint: What does it mean when the sea pulls back?

4. True or False: You should wait until you see the wave before you go to higher ground.

Hint: How fast do tsunamis travel?

5. True or False: Tsunami waves slow down as they get closer to the shore.

Hint: What happens to the waves as they reach shallower water?

Answers to Quiz 1:

1. False - A tsunami often consists of multiple waves that can arrive minutes to hours apart.

2. False - Tsunamis can also happen in large lakes and other large bodies of water.

3. False - If the water pulls back suddenly, it's a natural warning sign of an incoming tsunami, and you should move to higher ground immediately.

4. False - You should head to higher ground immediately after receiving a warning or noticing natural signs, without waiting to see the wave.

5. False - Tsunami waves actually gain speed and height as they reach shallower water near the shore.

Quiz 2: Multiple Choice Questions

Now let's try some multiple-choice questions! Read each question and choose the best answer from the options provided.

1. What should you do if you hear a tsunami warning?

- A) Keep playing or hanging out until you see the

water rise

- B) Immediately move to higher ground

- C) Call your friends to plan a beach party

- D) Wait for further instructions on TV or radio

2. Which of these is NOT a sign of a possible incoming tsunami?

- A) Earthquakes

- B) A rapid rise or fall in ocean levels

- C) Loud ocean noises

- D) A clear, sunny day

3. Where is the safest place to be during a tsunami?

- A) Near the shoreline to watch the waves

- B) On a boat in deep water

- C) In a tall, sturdy building on high ground

- D) In the basement of a beach house

4. How can communities prepare for a tsunami?

- A) Regular tsunami drills

- B) Building homes closer to the shore

- C) Ignoring tsunami warnings

- D) Avoiding all beaches

5. What should be included in an emergency kit for tsunamis?

- A) Toys and video games

- B) Water, non-perishable food, flashlight, and first aid supplies

- C) A collection of your favorite movies

- D) Beach equipment

Answers to Quiz 2:

1. B - Immediately move to higher ground is the correct action when a tsunami warning is issued.

2. D - A clear, sunny day is not a sign of a tsunami; tsunamis can occur regardless of the weather.

3. C - Being in a tall, sturdy building on high ground is safest during a tsunami.

4. A - Regular tsunami drills help communities prepare for a tsunami.

5. B - An emergency kit should include water, non-perishable food, a flashlight, and first aid supplies to ensure you're prepared for any emergency.

Quiz 3: Fill-in-the-Blanks

Fill in the blanks with the correct words to complete the sentences about tsunami safety.

1. If you feel an , one of the first things you should do is move away from the .

2. Tsunami waves are not like normal ocean waves; they behave more like a , flooding inland.

3. After a tsunami, it's important to stay updated with sources, like local or emergency broadcasts.

4. Rebuilding after a tsunami takes time, and it's important to build to withstand future tsunamis.

5. Education on tsunamis is important, especially for who live near coastlines to understand the risks and proper measures.

Answers for Quiz 3:

1. earthquake, coast
2. flood
3. reliable, radio
4. stronger
5. residents, safety

5 /
tsunami safety tips

how to stay safe

LEARNING how to stay safe in a tsunami is like having a magic cloak that keeps you invisible from danger. You easily protect yourself, your family, and your friends with this knowledge. By reading this guide, you can be ready for whatever comes your way. A tsunami may seem a bit scary, but your knowledge can keep you calm and smart. So sit back and read on to figure out how you can save yourself if one of those giant waves comes knocking.

1. Learn the Signs of a Tsunami

First up, being tsunami smart means knowing the warning signs. Sometimes nature gives us hints that a tsunami might be on the way. One big clue is an earthquake. If you feel the ground shake, act as though a tsunami could follow, especially if you're near the coast. Another sign is if you see the ocean water pull far back from the beach more than usual, which can happen minutes before a tsunami hits. These signs mean you need to act fast!

2. Know Your Escape Plan

Every superhero needs a good escape plan, and so do you! Make sure you know the quickest way to get to higher ground or inland, away from the beach. Most coastal areas at risk for tsunamis will have signs posted that show evacuation routes—follow them! If you're new to an area or visiting, take a few minutes to figure out where these routes are.

3. Practice Tsunami Drills

Just like fire drills at school, tsunami drills help you know what to do without having to think twice. Many schools and communities in tsunami-prone areas practice these drills. Participating in them helps everyone learn to react quickly and calmly. Remember, in a tsunami, time is precious, and practicing the drill can save precious minutes!

4. Have a Family Emergency Plan

Talk with your family about what to do if a tsunami warning is issued. Decide where you'll meet if you get separated and choose someone outside the area you can all contact to say you're safe. It's like having a family secret code for safety!

5. Keep an Emergency Kit Ready

Every hero needs their toolkit, and in the case of a tsunami, this means having an emergency kit. Your kit should have water, non-perishable food, a flashlight, a first aid kit, extra batteries, and some personal items like clothes and toiletries. Keep this kit somewhere you can grab it quickly if you have to leave home in a hurry.

6. Listen to Alerts and Warnings

When a tsunami warning is issued, your best source of information will be local radio, TV, or even alerts on your phone. These will give you updates about the tsunami and instructions from emergency services. Always listen to these messages and follow their advice —they're like the guidebook for your safety!

7. Stay Away from the Water

This one might sound obvious, but it's super important: stay away from the beach and any other areas close to the water. Tsunamis can pull things and people into the sea. Even if it seems like the water has calmed down, there might be more waves coming, so the safest place is somewhere high and dry.

8. After the Tsunami, Stay Put

Once you're in a safe place, stay there until officials say it's safe to leave. Sometimes, tsunamis can have multiple waves, and later ones could be bigger than the first. Plus, the area could be unsafe due to flooding and debris.

9. Help Others If You Can

If it's safe to do so, helping others can make a big difference. Sometimes, people might not understand the warnings or know what to do. If you can help friends, neighbors, or even pets safely, you'll be a real-life hero. Remember, teamwork is often what makes superheroes super!

10. Learn from Each Experience

Every tsunami is different, and there's always something new to learn. After things calm down, take some time to think about what happened and talk about it with your family or classmates. Could you have gotten to safety faster? Was your emergency kit missing anything? Learning from each event makes you even better prepared for the next.

emergency kit

You've learned a lot about tsunamis and how to be prepared. Now let's build an emergency kit together! Just like your adventure pack, this emergency kit includes everything you need to be ready for a tsunami or any emergency. So grab your pack, and let's be on our way!

What is an Emergency Kit?

An emergency kit is a collection of items you and your family may need in a sudden emergency. Since there might not be time to search for supplies when a tsunami is on its way, having everything packed and ready can make all the difference. It's like having a treasure chest that keeps you safe, prepared, and confident.

Choosing the Right Bag

First things first, you'll need a sturdy bag to hold all your items. A backpack works great because it's easy to carry, especially if you have to move quickly. Make sure it's comfortable to wear and has enough space for all your supplies.

Essential Supplies

Here's a list of the basic items every emergency kit should have:

1. Water: Pack at least one gallon of water per person per day, for at least three days. This will be used for drinking and sanitation.

2. Food: Include a three-day supply of non-perishable food items. Think of things that don't need cooking, like canned fruit, granola bars, peanut butter, and crackers.

3. First Aid Kit: Accidents can happen, so a first aid kit is crucial. Include band-aids, antiseptic wipes, gauze pads, adhesive tape, and pain relievers.

4. Flashlight and Extra Batteries: If the power goes out, you'll need a flashlight to see in the dark. Don't forget extra batteries!

5. Whistle: A whistle can help you signal for help if

you get separated from your family or if rescuers are nearby.

6. Dust Mask: This helps filter contaminated air, which can be crucial if the environment is dusty or smoky.

7. Plastic Sheeting and Duct Tape: These can be used to make an emergency shelter or to repair broken windows or doors.

8. Moist Towelettes, Garbage Bags, and Plastic Ties: For personal sanitation, these items are essential to keep clean and manage waste.

9. Wrench or Pliers: These tools can help you turn off utilities like water or gas if needed.

10. Local Maps: If GPS isn't available, paper maps can help you find evacuation routes and shelters.

Personal Items

In addition to the basics, you should also pack some personal items:

- Medications: If anyone in your family takes medication regularly, include a week's supply.

- Personal Documents: Pack copies of important documents like birth certificates, insurance policies, and identification cards. Keep them in a waterproof bag.

- Cash: If ATMs and credit card machines are down, having some cash can be very helpful.

- Emergency Contact Information: Write down phone numbers for family members, doctors, and local emergency services. Sometimes, cell phones don't work in emergencies!

- Comfort Items: Especially for younger adventurers, include a favorite stuffed animal, book, or a game. These can make the situation a little less scary.

Special Supplies for Pets

If you have pets, don't forget to prepare for their needs too:

- Food and Water: Include a three-day supply for each pet.

- Bowls and a Manual Can Opener: Make sure you can open pet food and serve it.

- Leash, Collar, and ID Tag: If you need to move quickly, these will help keep your pets safe and identified.

- Pet Carrier: If you need to evacuate, this will be essential for transporting your pet safely.

- Medications and Medical Records: Like humans, pets have health needs that shouldn't be ignored.

Maintaining Your Kit

Once your emergency kit is packed, keep it in a place that's easy to access in case you need to leave quickly. Check the supplies every six months to make sure everything is in working order and that food and medications haven't expired.

Practice Makes Perfect

Now that you have your emergency kit ready, why

not have a family meeting to discuss how to use each item? You could even make a game of finding the kit and practicing an evacuation plan. The more familiar you are with what to do and where things are, the more prepared you'll be if a real emergency happens.

safety checklist

Now that we have our go-bags packed, we need to know the steps for staying super safe in a tsunami or any huge emergency. This is more than just a list; it's your own personal superhero safety plan. By checking off each thing, you'll first be able to keep yourself from making mistakes, and in turn be better able to help your family stay calm and ready. Let's jump into the Safety Checklist and see how you can be your own hero!

1. Know the Signs of a Tsunami

- Earthquake: Remember, an earthquake can be the first sign of a possible tsunami if it happens under or near the ocean.

- Water Retreats: Watch if the ocean water pulls back unusually far from the beach, exposing the sea floor; this is a big warning sign!

- Strange Ocean Behavior: Any unusual behavior in the water could be a clue, like odd waves or a louder ocean sound.

2. Understand Your Local Tsunami Plan

- Evacuation Routes: Know and memorize the safest path to higher ground from your home, school, and any other place you frequently visit.

- Community Warnings: Learn what the tsunami warning signals sound like in your area (like sirens or alerts on your phone).

- Local Shelters: Know where the nearest safe shelters are located.

3. Make and Practice Your Family Emergency Plan

- Meeting Points: Decide on safe places to meet if you get separated from your family.

- Communication Plan: Have a list of emergency contacts, including family, friends, and local services, and know how to reach them if phones are down.

- Practice Drills: Run through evacuation drills with your family a few times a year.

4. Prepare and Maintain Your Emergency Kit

- Supplies Checked: Regularly check your emergency kit to make sure all items are in working order and not expired.

- Personalize Your Kit: Make sure your kit includes personal items like medications, glasses, or special foods if needed.

- Pet Supplies: If you have pets, ensure their food, water, and other supplies are also ready and accessible.

5. Stay Informed During an Emergency

- Listen to Local Authorities: Always follow the advice and instructions from local emergency officials.

- Stay Updated: Use a battery-powered radio or your phone (if still operational) to get updates about the tsunami or other emergencies.

- Check for Updates: If you are evacuated, check regularly to find out when it is safe to return home.

6. Know How to React When a Tsunami Hits

- Immediate Action: If you see any signs of a tsunami or receive an alert, move to higher ground immediately, even before official instructions if necessary.

- Avoid the Water: Stay away from the beach and any other water bodies.

- Stay on High Ground: Do not return to lower ground until it's declared safe by authorities.

7. Help Others If It's Safe

- Check on Neighbors: If it's safe, check on elderly neighbors or those who might need extra help preparing or evacuating.

- Community Support: Participate in community support efforts by sharing supplies or helping with clean-up when safe to do so.

- Share Information: If you have access to information that others don't, share it with them to ensure everyone is safe and informed.

8. Learn from Every Experience

- Discuss What Happened: After any drill or actual

emergency, talk with your family about what went well and what could be improved.

- Update Your Plans: Use what you learned to make your plans even better for next time.

- Stay Curious: Keep learning about tsunamis and safety. The more you know, the better prepared you'll be!

Printing this checklist and hanging it on your fridge, or keeping a copy in your emergency kit, can help remind you of what steps to take to be ready. By following these steps and checking off these actions, you'll not only keep yourself safe but you'll also be a big help to your family and friends during any emergency.

6 /
helping others understand tsunamis

WITH ALL THIS new knowledge about tsunamis and the best ways to be safe, let's find out what you've learned while giving you a chance to show off your creative side! We are going to make some Tsunami Safety Posters. Not only is making a poster a great visual reminder of all the things to do and not to do in the event of a tsunami, but it will also provide you with an opportunity to share with your friends and family what you have been studying. On top of all of that, it is fun to create artwork!

Materials You'll Need:

- Large poster board or construction paper

- Markers, crayons, or paint
- Stickers or stencils that fit the tsunami theme
- Glue and scissors
- Old magazines or printed images related to tsunamis and safety
- A ruler and a pencil

Step 1: Plan Your Design

Before you start drawing and pasting, take a moment to think about what you want to put on your poster. What are the most important things you learned about tsunami safety? You can draw a quick sketch with your pencil to plan where each part of your poster will go. Maybe you want to show what to do before, during, and after a tsunami, or perhaps you want to focus on the signs of a tsunami.

Step 2: Create Eye-Catching Sections

Divide your poster into sections to organize the information. Here are some ideas for sections you might include:

. . .

- Warning Signs: Draw symbols or pictures that show the warning signs of a tsunami, like the ocean retreating or the ground shaking.

- Safety Steps: List the steps to take in case of a tsunami, like moving to higher ground.

- Emergency Kit: Illustrate what should be in an emergency kit. You could draw each item or make a collage from pictures.

- Evacuation Plan: You could draw a simple map of your home or school area with arrows showing where to go.

Step 3: Adding Color and Labels

Use your markers, crayons, or paint to make your poster bright and colorful. Color can help make different sections stand out and make the whole poster more engaging. Don't forget to label each part clearly. You can use big, bold letters to ensure everyone who sees your poster can read it easily.

Step 4: Decorate with Extras

. . .

If you have stickers or stencils, you can use them to decorate the borders of your poster or to emphasize important points. This makes your poster not just informative but also visually appealing. You can cut out pictures from magazines that relate to your topic, like images of the ocean, people running to higher ground, or even emergency supplies.

Step 5: Review and Share

Once you're done, take a step back and look over your poster. Make sure you've included all the important information and that everything is spelled correctly. Ask yourself if your friends or younger siblings would understand the poster. If it's clear and complete, it's ready to share!

Where to Display Your Poster:

. . .

- In your classroom: Ask your teacher if you can display it in the classroom so all your classmates can learn from it.

- At home: Hang it up where your family can see it, like on the fridge or in the living room.

- In the community: Perhaps your local library or community center would let you display it so the whole community can learn more about tsunami safety.

Creating a Tsunami Safety Poster is a great way to use what you've learned and to help others be prepared too. Each time someone looks at your poster, they'll be reminded of what to do in case of a tsunami, which makes you a part of keeping your friends, family, and community safe.

7 /
the future of tsunami research

advancements in science

WE ARE GOING to investigate the progress of science and the impact it has made as we learn and defend ourselves from tsunamis. Every step forward made by science makes us a little more informed about when a tsunami may occur, how big it could be, and what we can do to defend ourselves.

Understanding Tsunamis Better

Long ago, people didn't understand much about tsunamis. They were mysterious and frightening because they seemed to come without warning. But scientists have been working hard to uncover their secrets, and now we know a lot more about what causes them and how they behave. Let's look at some of the cool advancements that have helped us along the way.

1. Seismic Monitoring: Listening to the Earth

Seismic monitoring has come a long way. Nowadays, scientists use networks of seismographs spread across the globe to detect earthquakes as soon as they happen. These instruments are super sensitive—they can pick up even the smallest tremble, whether it's under the ocean or deep within the Earth's crust. By quickly locating the epicenter and measuring the strength of an earthquake, scientists can predict whether it might cause a tsunami.

2. Deep-Ocean Sensors

One of the biggest advancements is the use of deep-ocean sensors, like the DART (Deep-ocean Assessment and Reporting of Tsunamis) system. These sensors sit on the ocean floor and detect changes in water pressure that indicate a tsunami is passing above them. They send this data to satellites in real time, giving scientists and emergency services a heads-up that a tsunami could be on the way.

3. Satellite Technology

Satellites are like the watchful eyes in the sky. They use radar to measure the height of the ocean surface very precisely. Changes in sea level, which might be caused by a tsunami wave, can be detected from space! This technology allows scientists to monitor tsunamis as they travel across the ocean, giving people more time to get to safety.

4. Computer Modeling

With powerful computers, scientists can take all the data they have—from seismic activity, ocean sensors, and satellites—and use it to model what might happen. These models can simulate different scenarios and predict where a tsunami might strike, how fast it will travel, and how destructive it could be. This helps everyone from city planners to emergency responders prepare more effectively.

5. Public Warning Systems

Thanks to advancements in technology, public warning systems have become more sophisticated. Today, people can receive tsunami warnings through various channels like TV, radio, smartphones, and even outdoor sirens. These systems are integrated with scientific data, so when a warning goes out, it's based on the latest and most accurate information.

6. Global Cooperation

Scientists around the world share data and research about tsunamis. This global cooperation means that when a tsunami is detected in one part of the world, countries thousands of miles away can be prepared. Organizations like the International Tsunami Information Center help coordinate this effort, making sure that the knowledge and data are shared quickly and effectively.

How These Advancements Help Us

All these scientific advancements mean that we can

be much safer when it comes to tsunamis. We know more about how to prepare, where to build, and when to evacuate. This makes our communities stronger and more resilient.

Be a Junior Scientist

Here's a fun activity: you can try being a junior scientist at home! With a parent or teacher, you can create a simple experiment to understand how waves work. Fill a large container with water and gently tap one side to make waves. Watch how they move and change as they hit objects like small toy houses or rocks. This can help you visualize a little bit of what scientists study about tsunamis.

Every day, scientists are working to learn more and to develop even better technologies to keep us safe from tsunamis. By staying curious and eager to learn, you can keep up with these exciting advancements. Who knows? Maybe one day, you'll contribute to this important field of science yourself!

how kids can help

Do you ever sit around and ask yourself how you, yes you, can make a big difference in tsunamis and other natural disasters? Then let's go! There are so many things you can do even if you are still young. Age is just a number, so just because you're not an adult does not mean you cannot help a lot of people stay safe and help your community stay prepared. Let's get started with this article to see how you can be involved in contributing.

1. Learn All About Tsunamis

The first step to being a great helper is to know your stuff. The more you learn about tsunamis—what causes them, how they behave, and how to prepare for them—the more you can help. You can read books, watch documentaries, and listen to science podcasts. By understanding tsunamis, you'll be able to explain them to others and why it's important to be prepared. Maybe you can even give a presentation in your class or start a science club at school!

2. Help Your Family Get Ready

One of the best ways you can help is by making sure your own family is prepared for a tsunami. You can:

- Help put together an emergency kit. Make sure it's stocked and ready, and maybe even decorate it to make it special.

- Learn the evacuation plan for your home and school, and practice it with your family.

- Make sure everyone knows where to find and how to turn off the water, gas, and electricity in your home because it might be needed during a disaster.

3. Be a Safety Ambassador

Teach your friends and neighbors what you've learned about tsunami safety. You could:

- Create flyers or posters to put up around your neighborhood or school.

- Help organize community drills. You could even volunteer to lead the drill or help others understand what to do.

- Start a safety newsletter with tips and news that you can share with your school and community.

4. Participate in Community Clean-Ups

After a tsunami or any natural disaster, communities need to clean up and rebuild. Even though you're young, you can help with:

- Beach clean-ups to keep your environment safe and clean.

- Helping to plant trees or restore dunes that can help protect the coast from future tsunamis.

- Organizing donation drives to collect food, clothes, and other necessities for those affected.

5. Use Your Tech Skills

If you're tech-savvy, there are cool ways you can contribute:

- Develop a simple app or a website with tips on disaster preparedness for kids.

- Make videos demonstrating safety tips and share them on social media or YouTube.

- Help the elderly in your community set up their devices to receive emergency alerts.

6. Be a Role Model

Even simple actions can show others how to be calm and prepared. Always listen to adults during drills and emergencies, follow instructions, and stay calm. By showing you can handle a scary situation, you help others feel brave too.

7. Encourage and Support Others

Sometimes, just being a friend can be a big help. After a disaster, people can feel scared, sad, or upset. You can:

- Make cards or write letters to cheer up other kids who have been through a disaster.

- Visit or volunteer at community centers where families are getting help.

- Offer to share your toys or books with kids who might have lost theirs.

8. Keep Learning and Sharing

Knowledge is powerful! Keep learning about tsunamis, the environment, and emergency preparedness. Share what you learn with everyone you know. The more informed people are, the safer they can be. And who knows? Maybe when you grow up, you might become a scientist, a policy maker, or a disaster response expert who can make even bigger changes.

simple experiments to understand water waves

Experiment 1: Create Your Own Waves

Materials:

- A large, clear plastic container (like an under-bed storage bin)

- Water

- Food coloring (optional)

- Small floating items (like rubber ducks or small plastic balls)

Instructions:

1. Fill the container about halfway with water. If you like, add a few drops of food coloring to make the water easier to see.

2. Place your small floating items on the water. These will help you see the movement of the waves.

3. Gently tap one side of the container to create waves. Watch how the waves move and how they affect the floating items.

4. Try tapping harder to make bigger waves and see what happens.

What You're Learning:

This experiment shows you how energy (from your tapping) creates waves in the water. Notice how the waves travel across the container and how they interact with the objects in the water. This is similar to how wind energy creates waves in the oceans and how those waves can move things in the water.

Experiment 2: The Impact of Wave Height and Water Depth

Materials:

- Two large, clear plastic containers

- Water

- A ruler

- A small ball or similar item to use as a wave maker

Instructions:

1. Fill one container with a lot of water and the other with just a little.

2. Drop the ball from the same height into each container and observe the waves that are created.

3. Use the ruler to measure the height of the waves in each container.

What You're Learning:

In this experiment, you're seeing how water depth affects wave height. The shallower the water, the higher the waves can be when impacted by the same force. This helps explain why tsunamis grow in height as they approach shallow coastal waters.

Experiment 3: Building a Miniature Beach

Materials:

- A large, clear plastic container

- Sand

- Water

- Pebbles and small sticks (for extra features)

- A spoon or small cup to create waves

Instructions:

1. At one end of your container, create a beach by sloping the sand down towards the other end.

2. Slowly add water until it covers the lower part of your sand slope, but not all of it.

3. Use a spoon or cup to gently create waves towards the beach.

4. Observe how the waves interact with the sand and any changes that occur on your miniature beach.

What You're Learning:

This experiment helps you see how waves affect the shorelines, like how they can erode beaches or build them up. It also shows how barriers (like pebbles and sticks) can protect certain areas from waves. This is similar to how coastal management works in real life to protect against erosion from ocean waves.

Experiment 4: Wave Reflection and Interference

Materials:

- A large, clear plastic container

- Water

- A few small, waterproof toys or blocks

Instructions:

1. Fill the container with water.

2. Place the toys or blocks at different places inside the container.

3. Create waves and watch how they reflect off the toys or blocks and interact with each other.

What You're Learning:

This experiment lets you see how waves can bounce off objects and how waves can meet and mix with each other. In real oceans, this can happen when waves hit islands, reefs, or the coastline, and it affects how energy is spread through the water.

glossary

1. Tsunami

   - What It Is: A series of ocean waves caused by large disturbances under the sea, such as earthquakes, volcanic eruptions, or underwater landslides. The word "tsunami" comes from Japanese and means "harbor wave."

2. Seismic Activity

   - What It Is: Movements within the Earth's crust that lead to earthquakes. It comes from the word "seismos," which is Greek for earthquake.

3. Earthquake

   - What It Is: A sudden shaking of the ground caused by the movement of the Earth's plates. Earthquakes can happen along faults, which are cracks in the Earth's surface where tectonic plates meet.

4. Tectonic Plates

- What They Are: Large pieces of the Earth's crust that fit together like a giant jigsaw puzzle. The movement of these plates can cause earthquakes, volcanic activity, and tsunamis.

5. Epicenter

- What It Is: The point on the Earth's surface directly above where an earthquake starts. This is usually the location where the earthquake is felt the strongest.

6. Magnitude

- What It Is: A measurement of the energy released during an earthquake, often described using the Richter scale. The higher the magnitude, the stronger the earthquake.

7. Richter Scale

- What It Is: A scale used to measure the strength or magnitude of an earthquake. Developed by Charles F. Richter in 1935, this scale helps scientists compare the size of earthquakes.

8. DART Systems (Deep-ocean Assessment and Reporting of Tsunamis)

- What It Is: A system of sensors placed on the ocean floor used to detect tsunamis. These sensors can measure changes in water pressure and send real-time data to scientists on land.

9. Buoy

- What It Is: A floating device in the ocean that can carry equipment for measuring weather and ocean conditions, including data important for detecting tsunamis.

10. Seismograph

- What It Is: An instrument that measures and records details about earthquakes, such as force and duration.

11. Satellite

- What It Is: A man-made object that orbits Earth and can be used for communications, weather monitoring, and in our case, detecting changes in sea level that might indicate a tsunami.

12. Wave Height

- What It Is: The vertical distance between the crest (top) of a wave and the trough (bottom) of the wave.

13. Crest
   - What It Is: The highest point of a wave.

14. Trough
   - What It Is: The lowest point of a wave.

15. Evacuation Route
   - What It Is: A planned, safe path that people follow to move away from danger during emergencies like tsunamis.

16. Emergency Kit
   - What It Is: A collection of essential items needed to survive and stay safe during and after an emergency. This kit usually includes water, food, first aid supplies, and other necessities.

17. Fault
   - What It Is: A crack in the Earth's crust where blocks of the crust move relative to each other. Movement along these faults can cause earthquakes.

18. Volcanic Eruption
   - What It Is: When magma (molten rock) and gases from below the Earth's crust escape to the surface, often explosively.

19. Underwater Landslide

- What It Is: A sudden movement of rock and soil down a slope under water. These can be caused by earthquakes and can trigger tsunamis.

20. Community Drills

- What They Are: Practice runs organized by communities to prepare for emergencies. These drills help people understand what to do and where to go during disasters like tsunamis.

further reading and resources

1. National Geographic Kids

   - What You'll Find: This site is packed with fascinating articles and stunning photos of natural phenomena, including tsunamis and other disasters. They break down complex topics into fun, easy-to-understand information.

   - Why It's Great: It's visually appealing and tailored for young learners, making learning about the Earth's wonders exciting and accessible.

   - Website: [National Geographic Kids](https://kids.nationalgeographic.com)

2. NOAA's SciJinks

   - What You'll Find: SciJinks is all about weather and Earth science. They have a section dedicated to tsunamis, with interactive diagrams, quizzes, and games.

- Why It's Great: It's made by NOAA (the National Oceanic and Atmospheric Administration), so you get super accurate and reliable info in a kid-friendly package.

- Website: [NOAA SciJinks](https://scijinks.gov/tsunami/)

3. BrainPOP

- What You'll Find: BrainPOP features short, animated videos on a multitude of subjects, including natural disasters like tsunamis. Each video comes with quizzes, activities, and related reading materials.

- Why It's Great: The videos are fun and engaging, perfect for explaining complex subjects in a simple way.

- Website: [BrainPOP](https://www.brainpop.com)

4. PBS Kids

- What You'll Find: PBS Kids offers videos and inter-active games that explore natural disasters. Their content is always educational and safe for children.

- Why It's Great: It integrates learning with fun inter-active content, great for younger kids.

- Website: [PBS Kids](https://pbskids.org)

5. The Disaster Duo

- What You'll Find: This YouTube channel features

two animated characters who teach kids about preparing for and understanding natural disasters, including tsunamis.

- Why It's Great: The videos are short, lively, and informative, making them easy to watch and learn from.

- YouTube Channel: Search for "The Disaster Duo" on YouTube.

6. BBC Bitesize

- What You'll Find: BBC Bitesize offers detailed lessons on various subjects, including geography topics like tsunamis and earthquakes. The site includes articles, videos, and infographics.

- Why It's Great: It provides a more in-depth look at how and why natural disasters occur, ideal for kids who are ready for more detailed explanations.

- Website: [BBC Bitesize](https://www.bbc.co.uk/bitesize)

7. Smithsonian Science Education Center

- What You'll Find: The Smithsonian offers a "Disaster Detector" game that helps kids learn to plan for and respond to natural disasters.

- Why It's Great: It teaches critical thinking and emergency preparedness through gameplay, which is both educational and entertaining.

- Website: [Smithsonian Science Education Center] (https://ssec.si.edu)

8. Kids Ahead - Wild Weather Adventure

- What You'll Find: This interactive game lets players explore different weather phenomena, including tsunamis, as they attempt to complete their missions.
- Why It's Great: It combines adventure and education, challenging kids to solve problems while learning about weather and natural disasters.
- Website: [Kids Ahead](http://www.kidsahead.com)

9. FEMA for Kids

- What You'll Find: This site teaches kids how to be prepared for disasters with information, tips, and strategies for safety.
- Why It's Great: It includes practical advice on what kids can actually do during different disasters, making them feel empowered and prepared.
- Website: [FEMA for Kids](https://www.ready.gov/kids)

10. TED-Ed Videos

- What You'll Find: TED-Ed has educational videos on a wide range of topics, including natural disasters. These videos often feature experts in the field and provide insightful, thought-provoking content.

- Why It's Great: TED-Ed videos are well-animated and scripted to provoke curiosity and deeper understanding.

- Website: [TED-Ed](https://ed.ted.com)

Made in the USA
Monee, IL
25 March 2025

14660969R00049